AVENGERS INFINITY WAR: THE ROAD TO INFINITY WAR: THE JOURNALS
A CENTUM BOOK 9781911461821
Published in Great Britain by Centum Books Ltd
This edition published 2018
1 3 5 7 9 10 8 6 4 2

MARVEL

© 2018 MARVEL

Centum Books Ltd, 20 Devon Square, Newton Abbot, Devon, TQ12 2HR, UK
books@centumbooksltd.co.uk

CENTUM BOOKS Limited Reg. No. 07641486

A CIP catalogue record for this book is available from the British Library

Printed in Italy

MARVEL

AVENGERS
INFINITY WAR

centum

PROLOGUE:

THE HERO: TONY STARK - AKA IRON MAN

WHEN IT ALL BEGAN...

There was a time when all I was interested in was **WEALTH and FAME.**

When I took over my father's business, STARK INDUSTRIES, I saw no reason not to continue down the same old well-paid path - manufacturing and selling weapons.

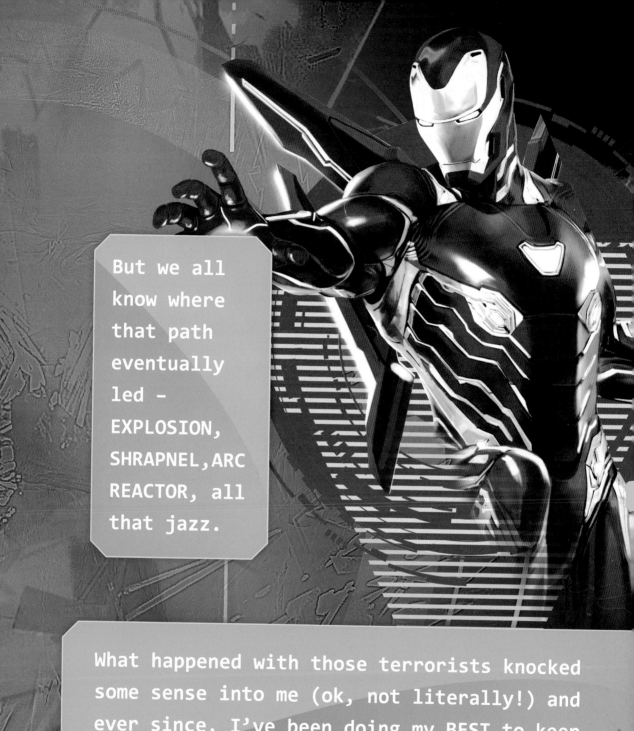

But we all know where that path eventually led - EXPLOSION, SHRAPNEL,ARC REACTOR, all that jazz.

What happened with those terrorists knocked some sense into me (ok, not literally!) and ever since, I've been doing my BEST to keep the world safe instead of aiding those who want to DESTROY it.

The Avengers have stopped THREAT after THREAT over the last few years but often in our attempt to PREVENT damage, we have CAUSED damage. HUGE damage. And so, the Accords. I really do believe the agreement was needed, though I hate the rift it has led to — THE DIVIDE BETWEEN MY AVENGERS TEAMMATES.

I know Steve Rogers, a.k.a. CAPTAIN AMERICA, ONLY wants to do good - he is a good man, the best - but he is on the WRONG SIDE here.

Doesn't mean I DON'T miss him though. Sin
that letter, I haven't heard another word
from him. Cap's gone UNDERGROUND. And as
tinker with armour in my lab, I can't hel
wondering WHERE HE IS RIGHT NOW, WHO HE'S
WITH, And WHAT HE'S UP TO...

NO MATTER what's happened, I can still count on STEVE R

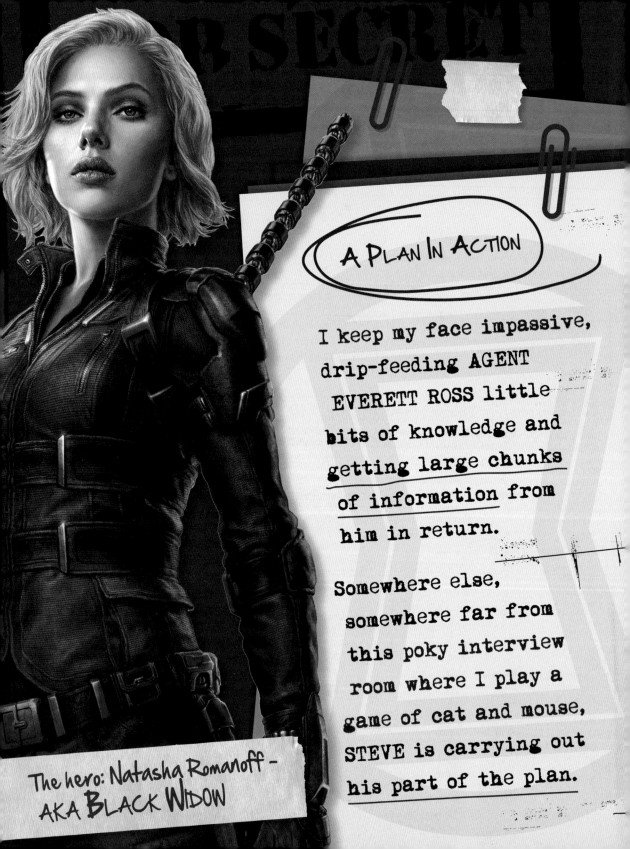

A PLAN IN ACTION

I keep my face impassive, drip-feeding AGENT EVERETT ROSS little bits of knowledge and getting large chunks of information from him in return.

Somewhere else, somewhere far from this poky interview room where I play a game of cat and mouse, STEVE is carrying out his part of the plan.

The hero: Natasha Romanoff – AKA BLACK WIDOW

ROSS WANTS TO KNOW WHY I DIDN'T STOP THEM — STEVE AND BARNES.

A smile on my face, I tell him I was just following orders. But I had known from the moment I let them go that there would be repercussions. There always were.

STEVE ROGERS

Steve knew it, too.

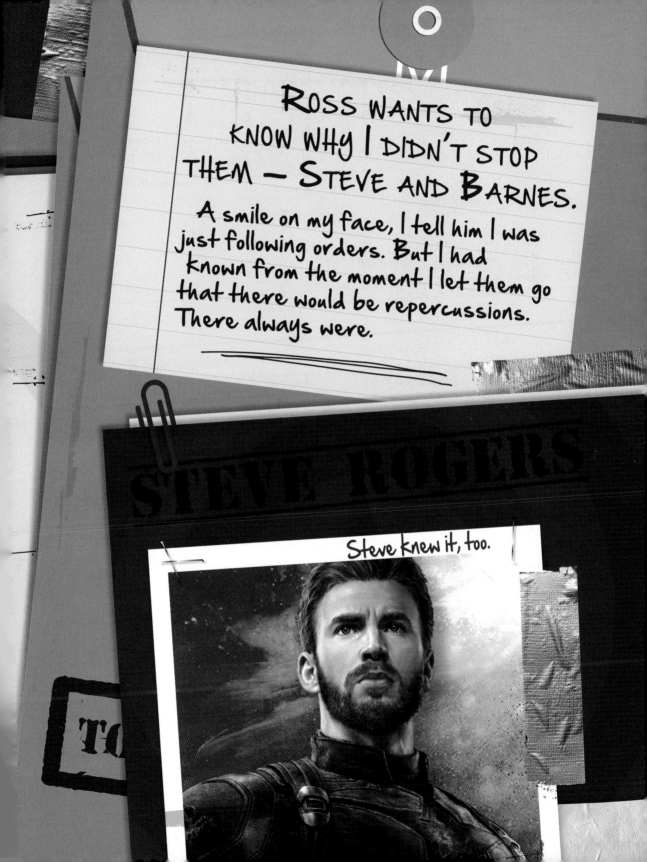

There was always a price to pay, and it was usually casualties and destruction. In New York. In Sokovia. In Nigeria, too. MY FELLOW AVENGERS AND I HAD LEARNED THAT THE HARD WAY.

TEAM IRON MAN

VISION

WAR MACHINE

BLACK PANTHER

BLACK WIDOW

And when LIVES ARE AT STAKE,
the government must take action.
The Sokovia Accords meant THE
AVENGERS could no longer operate
independently, instead we would be
supervised by the United Nations.

Tony felt it was a SMALL PRICE TO PAY in order to keep the Avengers together.

"WE'RE A PEACEKEEPING FORCE, SAME AS ANY OTHER."

— IRON MAN

The events of New York, Sokovia and Nigeria had weighed heavy on him and he tried to persuade the others to accept the Accords.

<u>STEVE COULD NOT.</u>

He worried that we would soon be told who was a threat and who was not and that THE AVENGERS could be used to serve a political agenda.

The possibility went against <u>everything</u> CAPTAIN AMERICA stood for.

And so the Avengers, once the <u>mightiest</u> team, were

DIVIDED.

AT THE TIME, BELIEVED ONY WAS RIGHT.

AT THE TIME.

AGENT ROSS wants me to 'do the right thing'. He says he knows I will.

And perhaps I will – I had a great teacher, after all.

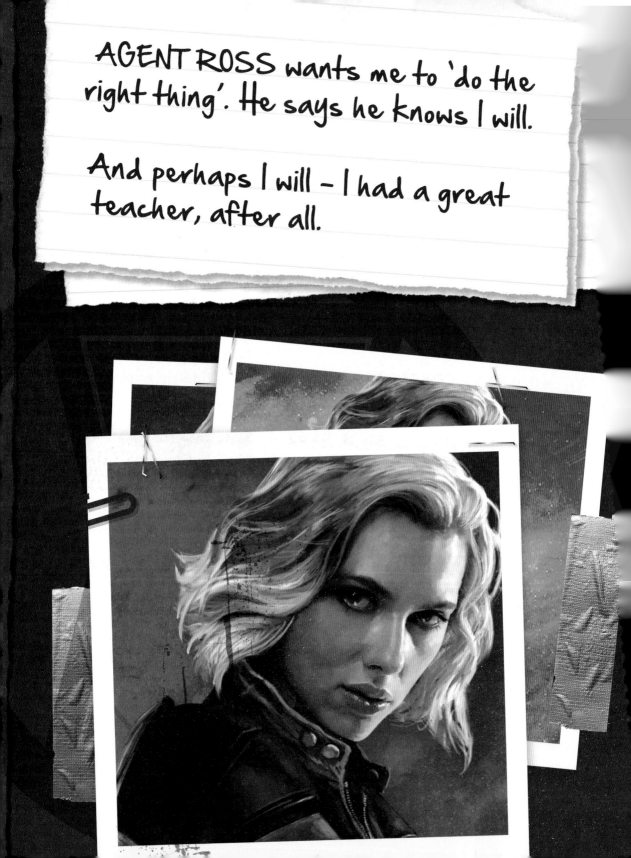

STEVE ROGERS

THE LEGENDARY 'FIRST AVENGER'.

Everyone knew STEVE'S STORY. Even me, growing up as a KGB recruit in deepest Russia.

In my dark, death-filled world, I would recall the stories I'd heard, as a tiny girl, of CAPTAIN AMERICA.

They were like fairy-tales of hope, telling me that there was such a thing as a truly good person.

But, I wondered, could a man of such consistent morality have ever REALLY EXISTED?

Eventually my talents as a SPY and ASSASSIN drew the attention of NICK FURY.

Thankfully, instead of being eliminated by S.H.E.I.L.D., I was recruited by them.

I had the chance of a NEW LIFE, one spent doing GOOD not EVIL.

And the opportunity to work alongside Steve Rogers.

I BECAME PART OF HIS STORY.

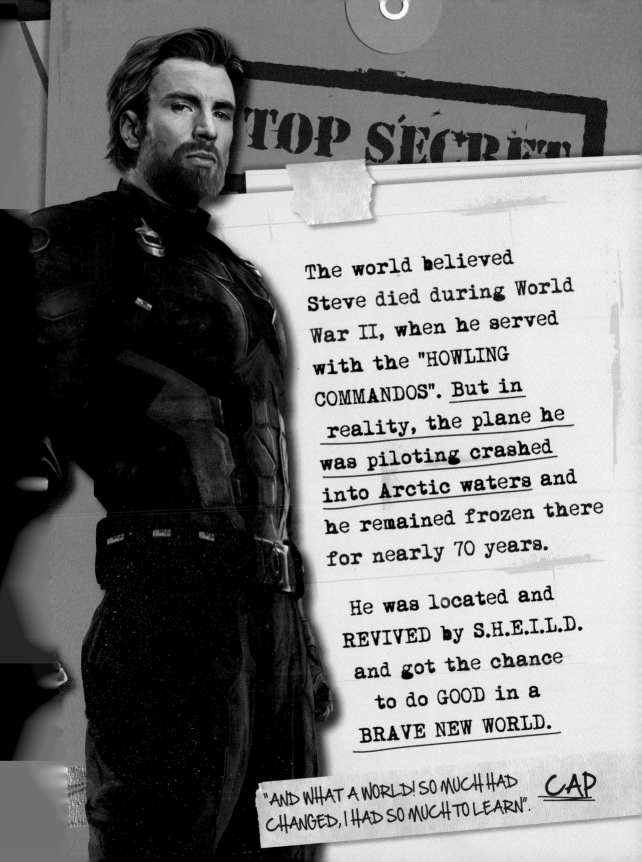

The world believed Steve died during World War II, when he served with the "HOWLING COMMANDOS". But in reality, the plane he was piloting crashed into Arctic waters and he remained frozen there for nearly 70 years.

He was located and REVIVED by S.H.E.I.L.D. and got the chance to do GOOD in a BRAVE NEW WORLD.

"AND WHAT A WORLD! SO MUCH HAD CHANGED, I HAD SO MUCH TO LEARN".

CAP

'BUCKY' BARNES

STEVE had suffered a GREAT LOSS during the war - the death of his best friend, James Buchanan 'BUCKY' BARNES.

OR AT LEAST HE THOUGHT HE HAD. It was the cruellest of hoaxes.

In fact, Barnes had
been experimented on,
brainwashed.

He became

THE WINTER
SOLDIER.

When Steve discovered this,
he couldn't just abandon his old
friend. He wanted to help him.

THAT WAS LOYALTY.

THAT WAS STEVE ROGERS.

Helmut Zemo had used that loyalty to try to DESTROY THE AVENGERS.

His plan had been to break up the Avengers from within, pit ally against ally, friend against friend.

Steve and Tony were <u>pitched against each other</u> when Zemo revealed that Barnes had been responsible for the DEATH OF STARK'S PARENTS.

Tony had wanted REVENGE on BARNES. Steve had been _unwilling_ to see his best friend killed for crimes that had been committed while he'd been 'brainwashed into being the Winter Soldier.

Zemo's plan had been a BRILLIANT one, causing the two Avengers to fight each other, seemingly to the death.

IT VERY _NEARLY_ SUCCEEDED, TOO.

After the battle between the heroes, between my FRIENDS, I had waited for Steve. When I finally got a call from him, plans were put in motion.

He needed my help and I agreed to give it, without question or reservation.

We are comrades, teammates, friends.

AND SO HERE I AM IN THE MIDST OF THAT PLAN.

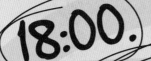

18:00.

Falcon, Ant-Man, Hawkeye and Scarlet Witch will all be safe by now. Steve will have freed them from the Raft.

And ROSS KNOWS IT.

SCARLET WITCH

Our little game is reaching its conclusion and there is only one more thing to discuss.

"Regardless of the Accords, the world needs THE AVENGERS."

Ross' words take me by surprise - not that you'd know it from my face.

Well good, because it's CRUNCH TIME.

I need co-ordinates to zero in on the chatter Steve and I have been picking up - and Ross has those co-ordinates.

"SO THAT'S WHAT YOU WERE UP TO, WHILE I WAS BUSTING SAM OUT OF THE STIR.."

CAP ⤴

IT'S NOW OR NEVER

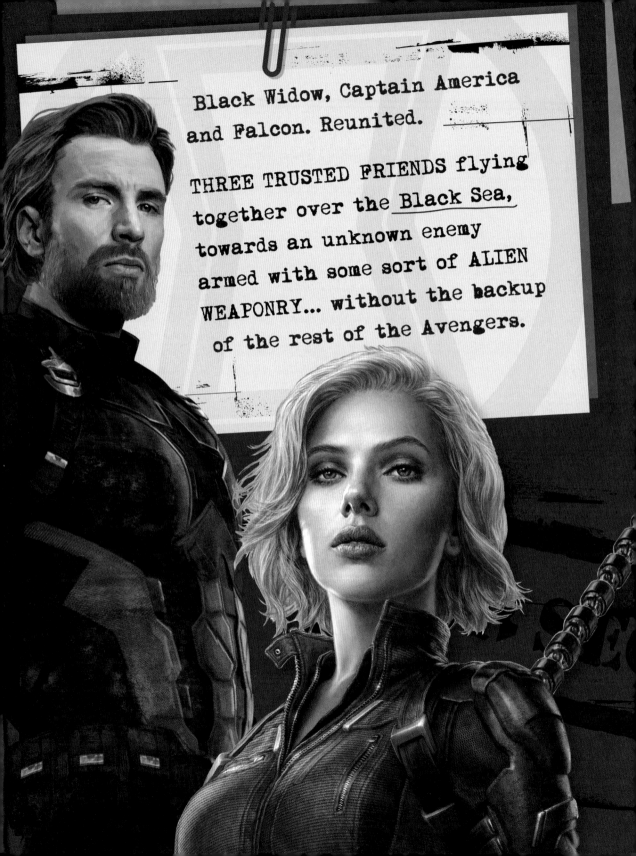

Black Widow, Captain America and Falcon. Reunited.

THREE TRUSTED FRIENDS flying together over the Black Sea, towards an unknown enemy armed with some sort of ALIEN WEAPONRY... without the backup of the rest of the Avengers.

FALCON

"Best mission EVER!"
Falcon

It's up to the three of us to save the world.
We can do it, I know we can, but it
would be a whole lot easier with the help
of the others.

I miss them. Especially Banner. I wonder
where Hulk is now... I hope he's with friends.

BATTLE FOR ASGARD

The hero - Heimdall - AKA Guardian of the Bifrost

THOR was with BANNER, the man who, when angered, turns into a green creature called HULK. I didn't know where they were, I couldn't see clearly enough at such a distance. I only knew that their paths had crossed for a reason and we needed Odinson to return to Asgard. IMMEDIATELY.

RAGNAROK WAS REAL AND IT HAD BEGUN.

It would mean the
END OF ASGARD

and all Asgardians.
Our only chance and
it was a small one,
was to work together,
THOR and I.

"WHEN YOU NEED HIM, HE WILL COME."

ODIN'S words echoed around my head.
I just hoped he was right.

"My brother. He makes much mischief."

THImage_refOR

"My brother. He makes much mischief."

THOR

I shouldn't blame LOKI, but as with all of the most recent threats to Asgard, this had been his fault. I should try to forgive him, as ODIN always did. But having seen what I have seen, FORGIVENESS WILL NOT COME EASY.

GUIDING THE PEOPLE OF ASGARD TOWARDS THE
BIFROST

in an attempt to SAVE them, I had thought back over LOKI'S previous misadventures and wondered for the millionth time,

WHAT COULD HAVE CAUSED HIM SUCH UNHAPPINESS?

Because only a DEEP UNHAPPINESS could have led him to do all that he has done.

SOME TIME AGO, three Frost Giants managed to enter Asgard unnoticed by me. They had been attempting to take back a relic – a weapon – called

THE CASKET OF ANCIENT WINTERS.

I HAD SENSED AT THE TIME THAT LOKI WAS INVOLVED, BUT COULD NOT PROVE IT.

THOR had journeyed over the Biforst to the frozen wastes of Jotunheim to demand answers from the king, LAUFEY. The mission was an unmitigated disaster and ODIN had been forced to step in before the Frost Giants attacked.

"They should have feared me, like they did my father!"

THOR

END RESULT

THOR'S BANISHMENT FROM ASGARD.

While THOR was consigned to Midgard, ODIN succumbed to the Odinsleep and LOKI became acting king of Asgard. He used his powers to freeze me, then activated the Bifrost and travelled to Jotunheim. It was then I knew for certain that LOKI'S CUNNING had been to blame for the failing of my senses.

UPON LOKI'S RETURN, having forged an alliance with LAUFEY, he ordered THE DESTROYER – a mobile, destructive weapon in the form of a man – to Earth to slay THOR. And I could only watch from afar, POWERLESS, as the Frost Giants invaded Asgard.

IN A SMALL TOWN ON EARTH, without his Asgardian might and his hammer Mjolnir, THOR faced down the Destroyer. His faithful companions SIF, FANDRAL, HOGUN and VOLSTAGG were by his side, but the Destroyer seemed unstoppable – until, from nowhere, MJOLNIR FLEW INTO THOR'S HAND.

ODINSON had proved himself worthy. The Destroyer was defeated, peace was restored and THOR was needed back on Asgard urgently.

I HAD TO ACTIVATE THE BIFROST.

The SAFETY of Asgard depended on it. Using all my strength and willpower to escape my icy prison, I brought THOR home to stop the Frost Giants.

"Big brother to the rescue again. OF COURSE."

LOKI

It turned out LOKI had played both sides. He attempted to
use the Bifrost to destroy Jotunheim and its people entirely.
Brother fought brother, until THOR SMASHED the
bridge with Mjolnir. THOR and LOKI were left clinging
on to the edge of the abyss.

ODIN emerged from the Odinsleep in time to grasp THOR. Despite LOKI'S betrayal, THOR still tried to save his brother. But LOKI did not wish to be saved.

"He is still my brother, WHATEVER his actions."

THOR

HE LET GO OF THOR'S HAND AND DISAPPEARED INTO THE DARKNESS.

FOLLOWING AN ENCOUNTER with Dark Elves, LOKI returned to Asgard. He cast an enchantment upon ODIN, wiping clean his memory, then deposited him on Midgard. Impersonating ODIN, LOKI assumed the throne. I had been fooled along with everyone else.

BRANDED A TRAITOR, I FLED THE CITY.

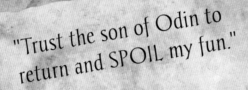

"Trust the son of Odin to return and SPOIL my fun."

LOKI

"Being overly dramatic as ALWAYS, brother?"

THOR

The ruse was only discovered months later, when THOR returned from Muspelheim bearing Surtur's crown. The brothers took the Bifrost to Earth in search of ODIN and that is where they encountered their sister HELA. ODIN met his end at her hands, as did Thor's trusted Mjolnir.

LOKI called for the Bifrost to be activated. THOR knew it was a mistake, but was too late to stop it. HELA arrived on Asgard – alone. And so began a terrible sequence of events, the GREAT THREAT that the Asgardians are fleeing from now.

"A MOST unwelcome guest."

Heimdall

WE WERE CLOSE, the bridge was within sight. It was quiet and empty, eerily so. But there was no time for doubt and I ushered them on. As the Asgardians HURRIED across the bridge, I had gazed past the mountains. To my relief, I saw that THOR had returned. He was distracting HELA and her army.

SUDDENLY there was a GRUNTING sound. Loud growls. A FENRIS WOLF, with fangs and glowing eyes. A long-dead creature, standing between all of Asgard and escape. It opened its mouth and began to run.

JUST AS ALL SEEMED LOST, two ships appeared in the sky. One began firing on the Fenris Wolf, halting its attack. The occupants of the ship were the HULK and a VALKYRIE. I had thought the ancient tribe lost, but thankfully it appeared not. The doors of the other ship, the larger ship, opened.

A rock-like creature beckoned the Asgardians on board, offering refuge. And behind him was LOKI.

"YOUR SAVIOUR HAD ARRIVED!"

LOKI

A GREEN GIANT, a VALKYRIE, a TALKING
ROCK, and the TWO SONS OF ODIN. A rag-tag
crew that were determined to prove themselves heroes.
To show that they were more than a match for HELA.
The SAVIOURS of the Asgardians.

BUT NOT OF ASGARD. I see now what I hadn't previously, even with my gift of sight – that **RAGNAROK** HAD to happen. Sacrifice the place to save the people. It was a brilliant plan and not one I could EVER have envisioned.

"Asgard is a PEOPLE, not a PLACE."

Heimdall

An Otherworldly Threat

I had envisioned an afternoon spent writing, but STEPHEN STRANGE has other ideas. He keeps popping into my study, bringing me tea and trying to peer over my shoulder.

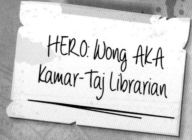

He's incredibly arrogant and incredibly annoying BUT I must admit, he has become an amusing companion. Not that I EVER let him know it.

"ONE day I will make you smile, Wong. ONE DAY!"
Doctor Strange

"Just a peek," Strange says. But when I REFUSE to play his game, or even engage in conversation, Strange gives up on extracting my thoughts and instead goes outside for a walk.

Finally, I am left in peace.

I CAN'T FOCUS ON MY WRITING!

I think back to when I first met Strange in Nepal. He had seemed even more arrogant to me back then, perhaps due to the brilliant career he had enjoyed as a neurosurgeon.

"Off-the-charts ARROGANT."

But that was BEFORE his accident.

On a rainy night, Strange's car had collided with another vehicle and CRASHED down an embankment. The impact had damaged the nerves in his hands, leaving him unable to hold a scalpel without shaking and making it IMPOSSIBLE for him to operate.

STRANGE'S CAREER WAS OVER AND HE FELT LIKE HE WAS NOTHING.

Strange searched for a cure, using all
his time and
almost all his
money, but
it seemed
hopeless.

UNTIL a man walked past him
in the street – a man who had been
paralyzed, who SHOULD have been
in a wheelchair.

The man told Strange about a place where, perhaps, a cure might be found.

THAT PLACE WAS IN **NEPAL.**

It was called Kamar-Taj. And it was where I was introduced to Strange by Mordo, a fellow disciple of The Ancient One.

Like me, Strange craved knowledge and devoured as many books as he could in the library. He even flipped through

"THE BOOK OF CAGLIOSTRO",

although I explained it was too advanced for anyone other than the Sorcerer Supreme.

Strange noticed pages had been torn out, so I told him the story of Kaecilius, a zealot who had a band of disciples. Together, they were attempting to bring to Earth a terrible being known as Dormammu, who dwells in the Dark Dimension. Kaecilius had stolen the pages, and removed the former librarian's head.

"Thank you for that HORRIFYING story, my friend."
Doctor Strange

But Strange had been dismissive of the teachings at Kamar-Taj, believing only in what he could see, touch, taste, hear or smell. When The Ancient One told him about the MULTIVERSE, he thought her a charlatan. Until she shoved his astral form right out of his body.

THEN
HE BEGAN TO OPEN HIS MIND TO THE POSSIBILITIES.

AND HE LEARNED QUICKLY.

Mordo and I found Strange in the library, reading *The Book of Cagliostro* and using the *Eye of Agamotto* to manipulate time. We were shocked and horrified at his RECKLESS use of such a POWERFUL relic – and more than a little impressed with his skills. Strange then demanded to know everything.

Sanctums in New York, London and Hong Kong create a protective shield around our world.

I explained that just as the Avengers protect from physical dangers, we sorcerers safeguard against mystical, metaphysical threats.

"The bill ALWAYS comes due."

I remember the words above well.

They were first spoken by Mordo. He was a man of great strength and courage, but he was also inflexible and believed in absolutes. I am wise enough to know there is much I do not know – the same could not be said of Mordo.

When Kaecilius and his zealots used a forbidden ritual to summon Dormammu to this world, I and the Hong Kong Sanctum fell.

When Strange and Mordo arrived and saw the destruction, Strange used the Eye of Agamotto to turn back time and save my life.

Strange then used the Eye to create an infinite time loop inside the Dark Dimension, trapping both himself and Dormammu within.

Dormammu killed Strange, but time rewound itself and so the confrontation happened over and over. Eventually, Dormammu agreed to leave the Earth alone, if Strange broke the **TIME LOOP**.

"I strike a GOOD bargain"
Doctor Strange

Mordo believed that Strange had violated the laws of nature, laws that are absolute. He wanted no part in it, felt he could no longer associate with Strange, or with me. He left Kamar-Taj and took off on his own.

"I was proud of Strange's INGENIOUS solution to a seemingly insurmountable problem"

This troubled me DEEPLY at the time and has continued to ever since. Mordo was a man of principle, and one who brooked no disagreement with his point of view.

COULD HE BE DANGEROUS?

AT LAST requiring a break from my memories, I head down the grand staircase. And find Strange standing at the bottom, rubbing his temples.

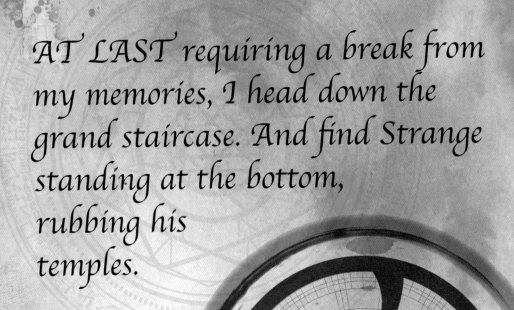

"I used to be a doctor. I knew how I was feeling WASN'T normal."

Doctor Strange

Together we head towards the Room of Relics and as we walk Strange tells me that he has been experiencing headaches and visions. He has seen something growing closer, a living thing that means to bring harm.

WHAT IT IS ISN'T YET CLEAR, BUT ITS DEADLY INTENT IS.

Doctor Strange

I have a horrible feeling that whatever Strange has seen will prove dangerous, and HARD to defeat.

There is SO much we don't yet know, so many terrifying things awaiting us out there in the cosmos. I believe that in the not-so-distant future, sorcerers and Super Heroes will need to unite if the universe is to survive. We must be ready.

WHAT MIGHT BE OUT THERE AWAITING US?

CODIFICATION
24780DTUKFJK-3458960-457821
456021378GHSDWGZXC-258932
000084327-DSHJKLN-234700021

SECRET

234756900%

A DAUGHTER'S REVENGE
THE HERO: NEBULA

There are many fearsome beings in the universe, but none more so than my father. Thanos, so huge he dwarfs his own throne, so frightening he can persuade anyone to do anything.

ACCESS LEVELS >> 2379044
YEOGDFGLJTRERXXVBTIEPW
35780-AKLEPQWETYU-7831

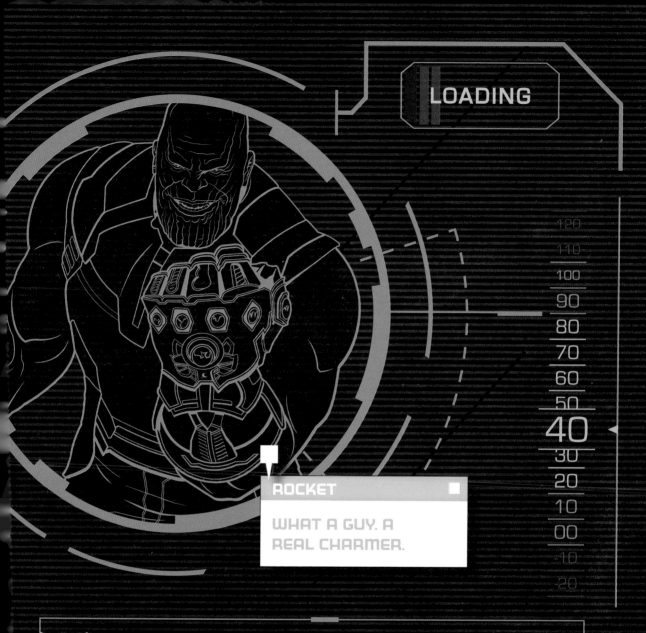

120
110
100
90
80
70
60
50
40
30
20
10
00
-10
-20

ROCKET

WHAT A GUY. A
REAL CHARMER.

> Fathers are supposed to make their children feel loved and
protected. Instead, Thanos instilled in me the emotions of
anger and fear. And over time, the feeling of rage grew and
grew until it all but consumed me.

1456YKLJH

35609000015608721
DSGHJKUETOLGYQWXC
GTPLZSAHJL23409568

SECRET

234756900%

Gamora was always his favourite. My sister, my enemy. You'd have thought our bond would be strong, having both been plucked from our families and thrown together. But no. Instead of standing together, I was forever behind her, left in her shadow.

> Fighting was what we did, Gamora and I. We spent day after day practising for battle, trying to win Thanos's praise. The winner got food, the loser got modified. But even when I won, I lost - as you can tell from my cybernetic arm. The rage grew.

LOADING

GAMORA

IT DIDN'T HAVE TO BE TH[IS]
WAY, SISTER.

24780DTUKFJK-3458960-457821
456021378GHSDWQGZXC-258932
000084327-DSHJKLN-234700021

SECRET

234756900%

ACCESS LEVELS >> 2379044
YEOGDFGLJTRERXXVBTIEPW
35780-AKLEPQWETYU-7831

245789V

When my sister and I were placed in the service of our father's emissary, Ronan the Accuser, there came an opportunity for me to finally prove that I was the strongest, the most skilled. Where others had failed, I could be the one to find the thing Thanos desired most, the Orb. It was somewhere on Xandar.

▶ Once again, Gamora stole the chance from me. She persuaded Ronan - and it didn't take much persuasion - that she could do the job quicker than me, she knew XANDAR better than me. Rage.

120
110
100
90
80
70
60
50
40
30
20
10
00
-10
-20

456YKLJH

35609000015608721
DSGHJKUETOLGYQWXC
GTPLZSAHJL23409568

CODIFICATION
24780DTUKFJK-3458960-457821
456021378GHSDWQZXC-258932
000084327-DSHJKLN-234700021

234756900%

But instead, Gamora was apprehended by the Nova Corps on Xandar and taken to the prison known as the Kyln. She had failed to return, but had she failed to locate the Orb? Together, Ronan and I headed to the Klyn to find out.

ACCESS LEVELS >> 2379044
YEOGDFGLJTRERXXVBTIEPW
35780-AKLEPQWETYU-7831

By the time we arrived at the prison, Gamora had escaped, along with an odd, rag-tag group she appeared to have joined. Had she - they - taken the Orb with them? I needed to find her and find out.

LOADING

120
110
100
90
80
70
60
50
40

NEBULA

LOOK AT THEM. BUNCH OF MISFITS. TOTAL LOSERS.

REPLY _ ROCKET

HEY! WHO DO YOU THINK YOU'RE TALKING ABOUT, BLUEY?

24780DTUKFJK-3458960-457821
456021378GHSDWGZXC-258932
000084327-DSHJKLN-234700021

234756900%

After a long and fruitless search, we received a transmission from Knowhere, a galactic outpost that was home to some of the galaxy's less reputable elements. One of Gamora's new friends, a tattooed individual called Drax, was vowing revenge on Ronan.

And if Drax was on Knowhere, then Gamora was on Knowhere, and so was the Orb.

ACCESS LEVELS >> 2379044
YEOGDFGLJTRERXXVBTIEPW
35780-AKLEPQWETYU-7831

120
110
100
90
80
70
60
50
40
30
20
10
0
-10
-20

DRAX

RONAN MUST FACE HIS DEATH!

As soon as we arrived, Drax confronted Ronan and I spotted Gamora escaping in a mining pod. I jumped in Ronan's ship, leaving him to take down Drax, and chased my sister through the sky.

Even under heavy fire, Gamora's pod didn't slow down. My heart beat faster at the thought of her escaping with the Orb - and my punishment at the hands of Thanos... It spurred me on and I fired again and again, until suddenly the pod burst into flames. Ignoring Gamora's lifeless body, I located the Orb and brought it aboard my ship.

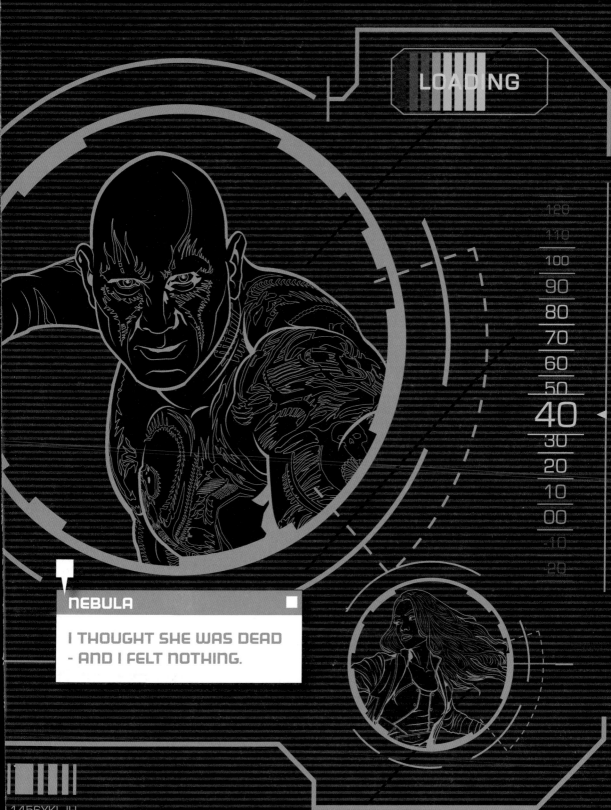

LOADING

NEBULA

I THOUGHT SHE WAS DEAD
- AND I FELT NOTHING.

CODIFICATION
24780DTUKFJK-3458960-457821
456021378GHSDWGZXC-258932
000084327-DSHJKLN-234700021

SECRET

234756900%

Instead of delivering the Orb to Thanos, Ronan decided to use its power himself to destroy Xandar. And if Ronan was prepared to defy Thanos, destroy him, then I would stand with him.

ACCESS LEVELS >> 2379044
YEOGDFGLJTRERXXVBTIEPW
35780-AKLEPQWETYU-7831

B9YDXZ-

120
110
100
90
80

ROCKET

IT WAS ME. I WAS LEADING THE RAVAGERS. BET YA DIDN'T SEE THAT COMING!

REPLY _ NEBULA

PESKY RODENT. I SHOULD HAVE KNOWN.

00
10
20

▶ But as we approached Xander, our ship was surrounded by Ravagers. They were associates of another of Gamora's new friends, Star-Lord. And if they stopped us from reaching Xander then Thanos would remain alive.

234756900%

The Ravagers blasted a hole in the side of our ship, then The Milano docked in the hole. Our ship had been breached. Gamora and her friends had boarded. And just before a huge blast hit me and knocked me out, I saw my sister approaching me...

GAMORA

YOU SHOULD HAVE FOUGHT WITH US, SISTER.

245789YDXZ-1

When I came to, we fought, Gamora and I.
Fiercely. I showed no mercy. But just as I
was about to finish her, the ship lurched
and I was flung backwards. My left wrist was
impaled on a spike, while the rest of my body
hung outside the ship. As Gamora reached
for me - to push me out, to pull me in? -
I severed my arm from my body. I heard my
sister scream as I fell.

120
110
100
90
80
70
60
50
40
30
20
10
00
-10
-20

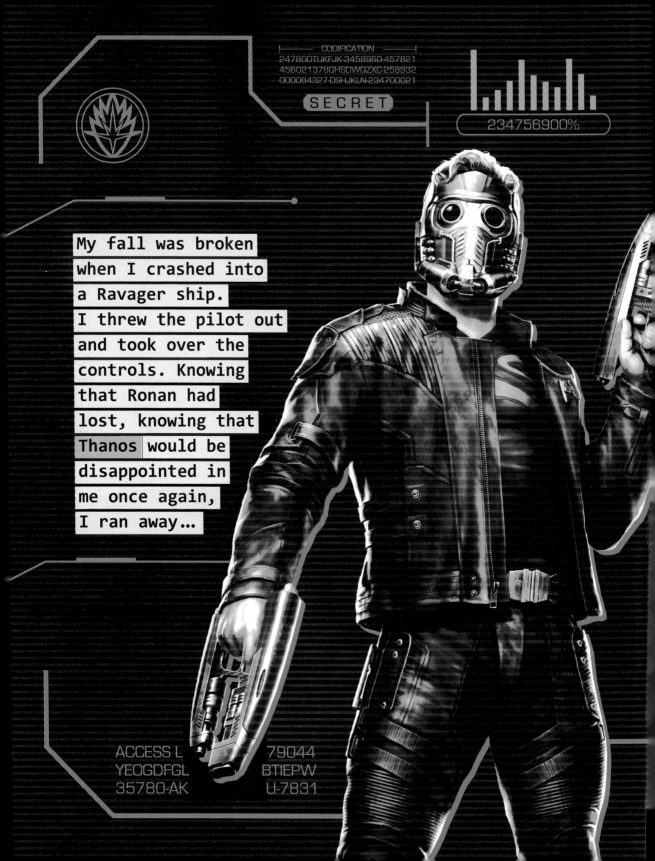

CODIFICATION
24780DTUKFJK-3458960-457821
456021378GHSDWGZXC-258932
000084327-DSHJKLN-234700021

SECRET

234756900%

My fall was broken
when I crashed into
a Ravager ship.
I threw the pilot out
and took over the
controls. Knowing
that Ronan had
lost, knowing that
Thanos would be
disappointed in
me once again,
I ran away...

ACCESS L   79044
YEOGDFGL   BTIEPW
35780-AK   U-7831

LOADING

120
110
100
90
80
70
60
50
40
30
20
10
00
-10
-20

▶ ...and was imprisoned by the Sovereign. Who released
me into the custody of Gamora. Who handcuffed me
to a railing in the crew's quarters of The Milano.
Which was where I was hanging when the ship was
attacked and crash-landed.

245789YDXZ-D2789-1456YKLJH

CODIFICATION
24780DTUKFJK-3458960-457821
456021378GHSDWQZXC-258932
000084327-DSHJKLN-234700021

SECRET

234756900%

Unfortunately, Gamora survived the crash. They all did. And as the rodent they call Rocket assessed the damage, an egg-shaped ship descended. It belonged to Ego, who is Star-Lord's father. Apparently.

So they all took off to planet Ego, leaving just me, the rodent and the plant. Almost as soon as they'd gone, we were attacked by Ravagers. I didn't feel bad about leaving Rocket and Groot to their fate and taking off in the Ravager's fastest ship.

120
110
100
90
80
70
60
50
40
30
20
10
00
10
20

ROCKET

DO ME A FAVOUR, WILL YA? STOP. CALLING. ME. RODENT.

1456YKLJH

CODIFICATION
24780DTUKFJK-3458960-457821
456021378GHSDWQZXC-258932
000084327-DSHJKLN-234700021

SECRET

234756900%

My goal was to end Gamora. But when I found her, chased her into a cave, exchanged blows with her, something happened to me. I realized that Thanos would never love me, would never be my true family. Only Gamora could fill that role. And so I let her go.

ACCESS LEVELS >> 2379044
YEOGDFGLJTRERXXVBTIEPW
35780-AKLEPQWETYU-7831

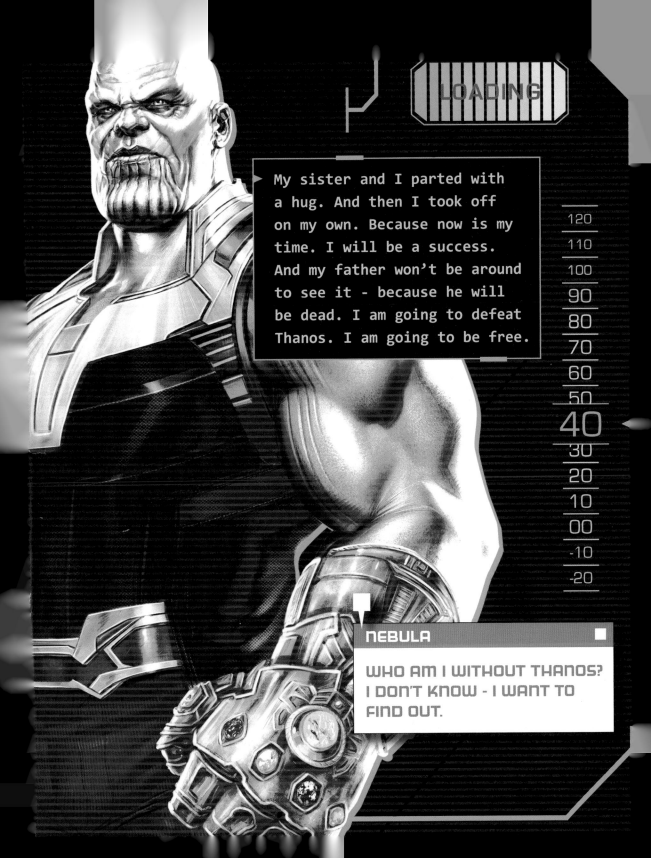

My sister and I parted with a hug. And then I took off on my own. Because now is my time. I will be a success. And my father won't be around to see it - because he will be dead. I am going to defeat Thanos. I am going to be free.

120
110
100
90
80
70
60
50
40
30
20
10
00
-10
-20

NEBULA

WHO AM I WITHOUT THANOS? I DON'T KNOW - I WANT TO FIND OUT.

EPILOGUE:

THE HERO: TONY STARK - AKA **IRON MAN**

WHAT NEXT?

BEING STUCK IN ALL THIS TRAFFIC MAKES ME RESTLESS. IT MAKES ME MISS FLYING.

THE FREEDOM OF IT. THE EXCITEMENT. PUSHING THE LIMITS.

Sometimes I almost touched the reaches of OUTER SPACE!

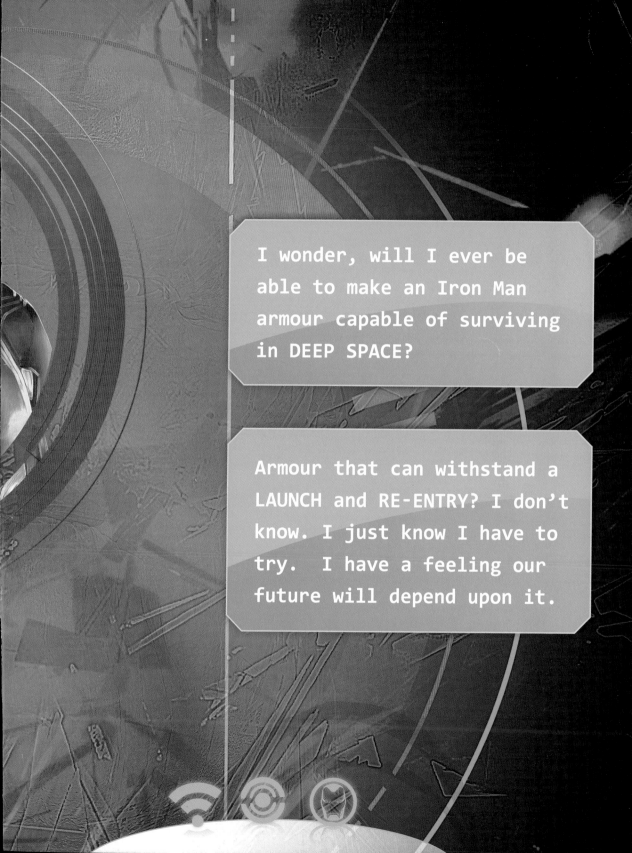

I wonder, will I ever be able to make an Iron Man armour capable of surviving in DEEP SPACE?

Armour that can withstand a LAUNCH and RE-ENTRY? I don't know. I just know I have to try. I have a feeling our future will depend upon it.

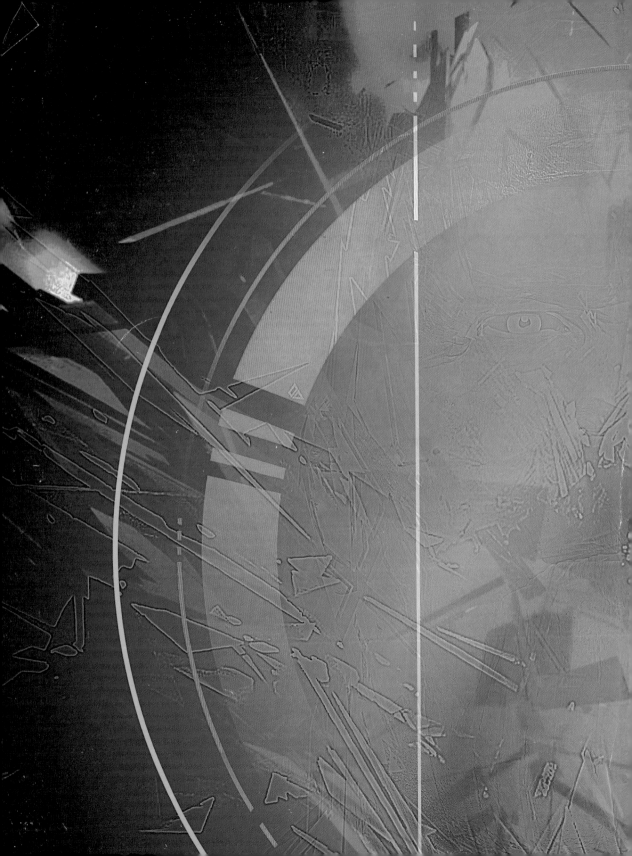